NIGEL CROSS

Virgin

ACKNOWLEDGEMENTS

The author would like to thank

Lynne Aldridge; Dave Massey;

Rachel; Jeff Horton; Pete Feenstra;

Richard Hoare; Colin Hill; Tasha Lee; Ian.

First published in 1997 by Virgin Books,

an imprint of Virgin Publishing Ltd

332 Ladbroke Grove, London W10 5AH

A catalogue record for this book is available from the British Library

ISBN: 0 7535 0196 1

Printed and bound by Graphicom, Italy

Designed by Ryanart

Dedicated to the memory of Randy California, a psychedelic fellow traveller

prologue

The air is a pungent mix of incense, sweat and anticipation. The audience is a frothing mass of idiot-dancing shapes and shadows. Slowly a hand rises out of the mist and a flower – a sunflower – is passed over to the stage. Up on the boards a thousand candles flicker, picking out the silhouettes of a four-piece rock band – drummer, organist, bass player and guitarist – against a pulsating coloured backdrop. Over the heavy beat, the organist karates out a surging wave of Hammond magic.

The blond-haired guitarist, meanwhile, stamps his foot down on an array of electronic pedals and swaying up to the microphone sacredly intones in Sanskrit, 'acintya bheda bheda tattva'. The audience takes up the holy chant as if it were some sort of tribal religious gathering.

You'd be forgiven for thinking that this was a scene taken straight from a psychedelic dungeon like Chalk Farm's Roundhouse at the fag end of the 60s and the group up on the stage was Steppenwolf or Traffic. In fact it was the scene at Kula Shaker's appearance at the MTV Awards at London's Alexandra Palace in September 1996. Seemingly materializing out of nowhere, this quartet has come to dominate the late 90s UK rock scene, and unlike contemporaries such as Oasis pay no lip service to the all pervasive rave culture or more strangely to the god punk. 1996 was Kula Shaker's year – everyone from 30-something jazz-funk smoothies to 90s teenage flower children snapped up their debut album K and turned it into a platinum-selling monster that's been praised by individuals as diverse as ginger-topped DJ Chris Evans to man of the moment Noel Gallagher of Oasis. Just when Britpop was looking dog-eared and jaded and some of its main proponents were showing distinct signs of

dwindling inspiration, Kula Shaker's
revved-up guitar rock with a twist of
Eastern delight blew the sweet breeze of
the Orient through its sagging sails.

Kula Shaker are men with a mission.
Not content to sit back and wallow in the
nineties new lad 'birds'n'booze' mentality,
the band are seriously looking at ways to
step beyond the one-dimensional rock
'n'roll lifestyle. As they hurtle towards the
year 2000, they intend to communicate
their concerns and blueprint for survival
of the planet as a whole. The band are
serious students of Eastern mysticism,
numerology, Vedic astrology, reincarnation and vegetarianism, but their aim is to
strike the social nerve of the masses.
They've got a world view. It's no joke that
they're all big fans of late-60s' rock – and
it isn't enough for them to just assume its
1967 candy-striped wardrobe and re-create its rainbow-hued sounds, although
they do this convincingly.

The years between 1966 to 1969
saw a period when music meant more
than money and hedonism. It was a time

of massive social upheaval and spiritual change. An era when rock icons from Lennon to Jagger, Hendrix to Morrison momentarily tried to offer an alternative to the burnt-out politicians promoting a spiritually bankrupt system. Kula Shaker have taken up that much-reviled baton. They want to achieve more than just

hoist the image of those long-gone icons like a gigantic stage prop. While the band doesn't disregard the musical influence of the 60s, or even the 70s, they intend their music to lead the way forward, not point backwards.

While bands like Ocean Colour Scene and Oasis seem happy enough to relocate themselves in their parents' record collections, Kula Shaker are one step ahead of the posse. They're aiming, leader Crispian Mills states, to bring about social change through the message in their music. As to whether it's just an idle boast that they'll complete the 'revolution', so optimistically promised 30 years ago but never delivered by those revered predecessors, only time will tell, but their star is dizzyingly in the ascent and their potential infinite. Only the imminent Armageddon they consistently talk of looks like putting a crimp in a career that's already etched with magic and mysticism, coincidence and conspiracy theory . . .

Kula Shaker are no 90s hippies – they see themselves as latterday knights setting out to reclaim the Holy Grail . . . their magical mystery tour has so far been a long and strange one, packed with enough action to satisfy even the most ardent Arthurian pilgrim!

Ocean Colour Scene

knights of the road

Charismatic singer – guitarist, Crispian Mills, he of the elfin stature, high-cheekbone good looks and honey-coloured shag haircut, not to mention loquacious bent, must have secretly always known he was bound for a glorious career. Though he doesn't like to talk about it, Crispian's a scion of one of Britain's most famous movie dynasties, the Mills family. A Capricorn, born 18 January 1973, Kula's front-man-to-be grew up in a genuinely serious thespian atmosphere.

His mother, Hayley Mills, had enjoyed an almost idyllic career as a child star for Disney (Pollyanna, In Search Of The Castaways, The Moonspinners) before going on to more mature roles as the classic Swinging London actress in films such as Twisted Nerve, via a teenage role in the much-loved Whistle Down The Wind.

His aunt Juliet was also an actress, as was grandmother Mary. His father, director Roy Boulting, member of another famous English family with cel-luloid connections, left home when Crispian was two and is not someone Mills is happy to recall, which is why he doesn't use his name. Boulting was married six times, and Crispian was his seventh son. The role of stepfather was taken over by Leigh

The Mills family

Lawson, a gritty, street-sussed actor from Coventry, which meant that Crispian's early years were split between the family seat in the decidedly posh suburb of Hampton in south-west London, and the more down-to-earth and less glamourous West Midlands.

But it was the bloodline to his maternal grandfather, Sir John Mills, which perhaps explained his attraction to the musical spotlight. In the 40s and 50s, John Mills became the epitome of the stiff-upper-lip Englishman with chivalrous and conscientious values in feature-film roles as diverse as Shorty Blake in In Which We Serve or as the courageous eponymous hero of Scott Of The Antarctic.

Crispian was born shortly after his grandad had been awarded an Oscar for his portrayal of the village idiot Michael in David Lean's critically acclaimed Ryan's Daughter, though few people know that Sir John had actually started out his career as a song and dance man in musical comedy in the 30s! However, it was Hayley who accidentally put him on the road to spiritual enlightenment when she took him to a Hare Krishna Temple in Watford when he was about 11. Though the youngster was impressed by the powerful energy he felt there, the acolytes in their robes at first struck him as weird and he wanted to escape. However, the experience changed his view of the world completely, and he began to see that what he had previously taken to be normal was weird, and vice versa.

Eleven was the age he also underwent another key experience — it's no wonder the number has become such a significant one for him. He discovered mortality, as he told Q magazine, 'If I ever had a Road-To-Damascus, it was when I was 11. I woke up one night at home in bed and realised I was going to die. I don't mean "tomorrow" or "in a year". It wasn't a prediction. It was just suddenly understanding fully that death would come. I remember talking about it at the time. Everyone thought there was something wrong with me'.

His natural inquisitiveness soon led him to make other discoveries such as finding a copy of the epic Indian classical poem, The Mahabharata – especially the section 'Bhagavad-gita', which further opened his adolescent eyes to a spiritually fulfilling future. The book was to stay with him and play its part in the subsequent Kula Shaker story. He also discovered the joys of vegetarianism, even if his first forays into alternative cuisine were only to impress a girl he fancied!

Significantly, rock music, and 60s vintage at that, was also about to enter his life – one day during a holiday from boarding school, he walked into the living room to be laid flat by the Kinks' garage bone-shaker, 'You Really Got Me' and life would never be the same again. Crispian had grown up listening to Duran Duran and Boy George on the radio, but 'You Really Got Me' hit a nerve and inspired in him a fierce determination to become a brilliant guitarist. He practised playing, studied tapes and listened to the Rolling Stones, Deep Purple and Ritchie Blackmore.

Indeed the black knight of the Stratocaster became something of an obsession with the budding guitarist, as he later admitted to Guitar Magazine. 'I'm a huge Ritchie Blackmore fan. He played all that mad fast lead guitar, but it was really sloppy and had a kind of garage feel about it. When I first heard 'Highway Star', it was like "Wow! Beethoven, man."' Ritchie wasn't the only British six-string bender to ignite Crispian's volatile teen imagination, Led Zeppelin's Jimmy Page exercising equal fascination.

Crispian's ambitions to become the next axe god were put on hold when he was packed off to that great leveller of teenage optimism, public school — and like certain other of his later rock contemporaries such as Thom Yorke from Radiohead, he spent a tough period incarcerated in this fine English educational institution, in his case at Stowe.

Mills only made it through 12 months there before he'd reached the end of his tether. 'I went to my mum', he told Q, 'and said, "I'm out. If you make me stay there any longer, I'm gonna become a communist"'. Back in a comprehensive in West London, Crispian resumed his aim to become one of the world's greatest guitar players, with a missionary zeal.

At 15, he suddenly became obsessed with the wah-wah pedal, and when the Stone Roses' 'Fool's Gold' came out with lots of wah-wah pedal on it he felt as if he had become fashionable for a while. After a decade of anti-rock sentiments, bands like the Smiths, sequencers and house, the Roses suddenly made the electric guitar the kind of appendage every young boy in the land wanted — rock was back and it was very psychedelic, even if the inspiration was ecstasy rather than lysergic acid. Without the example of the Roses, there'd have been none of the excitement, craziness and mayhem of late 90s British rock.

Around the time the Roses were shaking audiences up in the North of England, Crispian enrolled at Richmond College — a fortuitous move. In 1988 he met Alonza Bevan there, the power behind the Kula throne, the yang to Mills's yin and the right-hand man in all the guitarist's musical ventures to date. A Scorpio, Bevan was born in the year of the dog in West London on 24 October 1970 to Welsh parents. Hence his nickname of Shep, apparently because he's really a border collie in humanoid form!

Folklore has it that Alonza and Crispian met in a local park, Bevan was reading a book of Shelley's poetry and Mills fell into conversation with him.

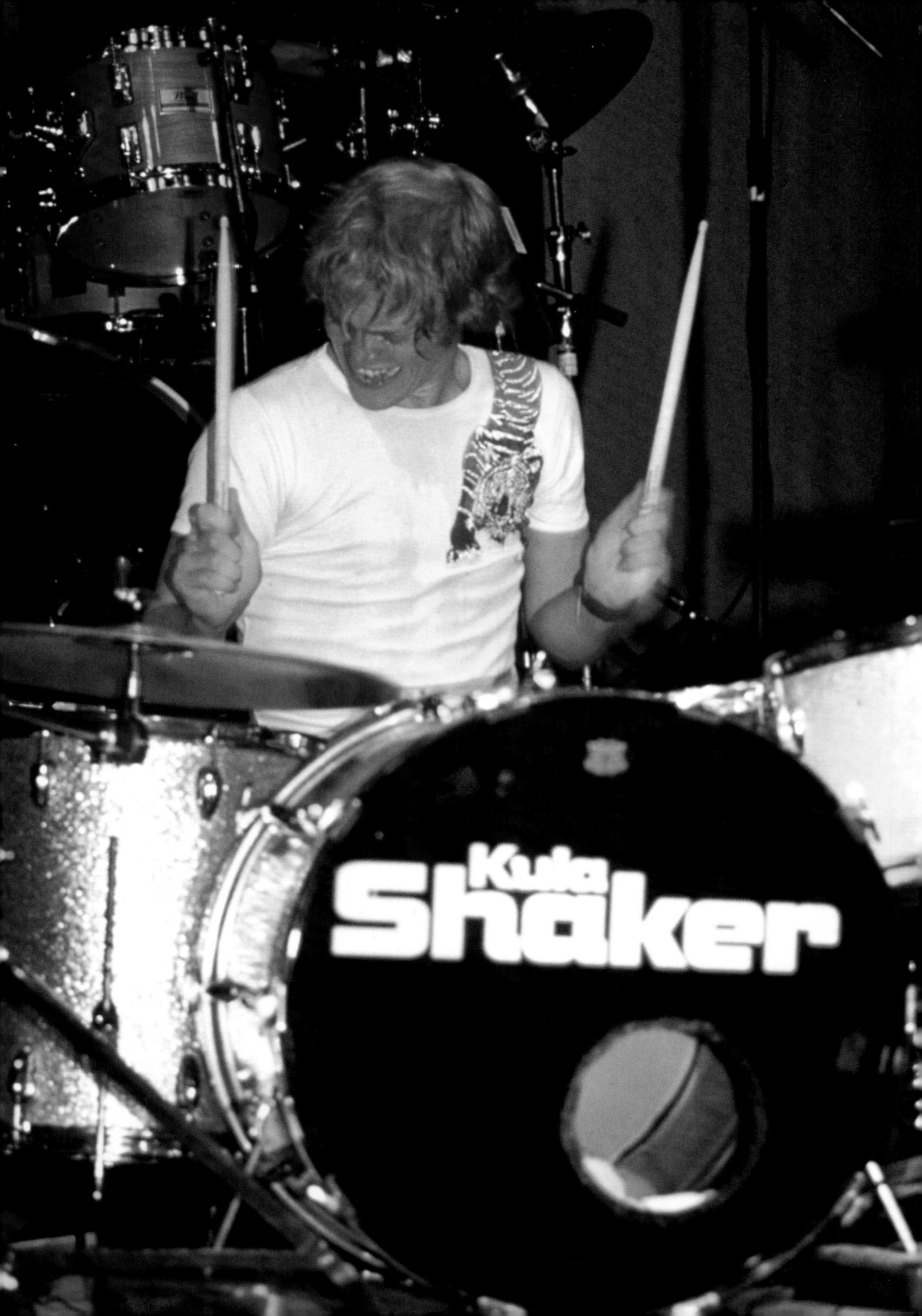
Kula
Shaker

Within the day they felt they'd known each other all their lives, discovering a common obsession with the Grail legend and the prophecy that King Arthur would soon return to inaugurate the Golden Age at England's greatest hour of need. It wasn't long before the pair found out that they also held a mutual interest in music and before you could say 'Jumpin' Jack Flash', they'd signed up with a local psychedelic band, called the Objects Of Desire, led by frontman Marcus Maclaine.

Above: The Beatles
Right: The Small Faces

However their ambitions weren't confined to twanging the strings of their electric guitars and, before long, they involved themselves in running a club, the Mantra Shack at Richmond's Ice Rink, where a new generation of paisley-shirted beat-teens could groove to the likes of Dr Phibes And The House Of Wax Equations or even the emergent Dodgy. Crispian later explained how surreal the club was. People would come out of the club and find themselves in the middle of a light-show in an ice rink complete with organ playing.

In the mid 90s psychedelic music has once again become a hip by-word for cool, but back in the days of the Mantra Shack it was a dirty word. Psychedelic music probably had its origins in the West Coast of America youth culture of the mid-60s — the West Coast had always been a bohemian centre for jazz

musicians and second home for the 50s beat poets such as Kerouac and Ginsberg. Marijuana was always rife and in the early 60s LSD was still legal, with the US government actually experimenting on human guinea pigs.

These tests gave novelist and scene-maker Ken Kesey the idea to hold 'acid tests' with audiences coming together to take the LSD sacrament and groove to its effects against the backdrop of electric pop, provided by a San Francisco beat band called the Warlocks, who later became one of the era's most celebrated rock icons, the famous Grateful Dead.

While Kesey and his merry band of pranksters cranked up the psychedelic scene in north California, in Los Angeles, bands spearheaded by the

Byrds were also experimenting with hallucinogenic drugs and electric sounds, culminating in what was probably the first bona fide psychedelic pop song, 'Eight Miles High'. The Byrds turned on the Beatles, and by 1967 the acid-rock culture had spread around the world via the likes of the Yardbirds, the Jimi Hendrix Experience, the Pink Floyd and the Beatles' call to arms, Sgt Pepper. Musicians used all kinds of effects to simulate what it was like to take an acid trip, using distortion pedals, backwards tapes, guitar feedback, keyboard innovations like mellotrons, and new, unearthly re-creations of orchestral strings, and a tape-loop effect dreamed up by engineer George Chkiantz called phasing that sent songs like Nirvana's 'Rainbow Chaser' and the Small Faces 'Itchycoo Park' into the ether. Indeed the Small Faces more than most bands

recognized the supposed beneficial effects of LSD and the quartet consumed copious amounts of the drug which resulted in one of the era's most startling and creative albums of the time, Ogden's Nut Gone Flake.

Meanwhile records like the Yardbirds' 'Happenings Ten Years Times Ago' and the Doors' dark musing on Oedipal love, 'The End' took rock into areas far beyond the clean cut pop song of the 50s. However, the late 60s sense of experimentation with organic drugs and their effects on rock began to sour into pompous progressive rock, heavy metal, concept albums and excessive use of euphoriants such as alcohol, coke and heroin as enjoyed by the likes of the late Keith Moon and John Bonham in the early 70s. Psychedelia began to fall out of favour especially with the onslaught of punk, despite the likes of some of its original exponents such as the Floyd's Syd Barrett and the Thirteenth Floor Elevators' Roky Erickson being name-dropped by everyone from John Lydon to Captain Sensible.

In the 80s, in the UK especially, as the anti-rock witch trials shook up the establishment, psychedelic rock was in short supply, and you had to cleverly subvert it – as did Julian Cope and his cronies in the Teardrop Explodes successfully did to make it palatable to both new audiences and jaded rock hacks, though certain camps were predicting a comeback.

As the late-lamented pop weekly Sounds pondered in the spring of 1984 – was there a psychedelic revival imminent? A special issue given over to this theory seemed to suggest it was a true underground happening, coming together from very diverse cliques: there was the Mod psychedelic subculture

of the Mood 6 and the Carnaby Street 'Splash Of Colour' scene, the Clinic and the Doctor, reissue labels like Bam Caruso trying to meticulously re-create the style and quality of 60s labels like Elektra, beat bands like the Prisoners and the Playn Jayne, the LA paisley underground that spawned the highly influential Rain Parade, and outfits like the 3 O'Clock, Australian garage bands of the calibre the Lime Spiders and the Moffs, Milwaukee's Plasticland, Baltimore's United States Of Existence, The Nomads in Sweden, and spoof bands like Naz Nomad & The Nightmares (a psyche off-shoot of the Damned) and the Dukes Of Stratosphear (XTC's amazingly authentic 60s side-tryp) — and there was an explosion of fanzines which wanted to fan the flames.

Sadly the media shunned, even ridiculed the notion but the timing was wrong and the moment lost to the advent of rave culture. Bands such as the Bevis Frond and the Sun Dial enjoyed cult acclaim and occasionally figureheads such as Bobby Gillespie would spout words of wisdom about stellar key psychedelic influences like The Misunderstood from Southern California, while his band's Screamadelica album was one of a handful of genuine attempts to fuse rock with house and show that there were more than just a few superfi-

cial similarities between late 60s tribal gatherings and late 80s raves. And underground the psychedelic tea-pot bubbled on via bands like the Treatment and fanzines like the Freakbeat.

Occasionally acts would even get into the mainstream, like the Shamen, who started out marrying 60s psychedelia with political and spiritual mediations and then crossed over into the 90s techno scene to become a major force. Yep, the Objects Of Desire weren't exactly working out of a void.

A hard-core slowly began to evolve when the band was joined by drummer Paul Winter-Hart in 1991, a Libra born on the 19 September 1971 in one of the most spiritual corners of the British Isles — Ynis Witrin, aka Glastonbury. Now most people recognize the Somerset town as the site of the UK's grooviest, most mind-blowing annual gathering, where people have traditionally come together to celebrate the summer solstice and three days of hot rock'n'roll and unbridled hedonism. But this town in the Mendips is widely regarded as one of this country's most sacred sites — rumoured to be the place where Joseph of Aramathea brought a phial of Christ's blood after the Crucifixion and a site equalled only by Stonehenge in pagan folklore.

Indeed it's been described as the place where King Arthur located his Camelot and is still regarded as the centre of one of the country's most powerful configurations of ley-lines which converge on the Tor. Like the rest of Kula, Paul was reared in something of an artistic atmosphere — though he'd discount the post-hippy, New Age vibes that have hung over Glastonbury since 1970 when the first Festival took place in the west of England. Paul's dad was a jazz drummer who gave his son a lot of New Orleans records, and by the time he had reached the age of 14, Paul had truly discovered a desire to be behind the traps.

Early influences included John Bonham, Mitch Mitchell and, surprisingly, funky Little Feat sticksman Richie Hayward, who'd also played in one of the late-60s' most far-out outfits, The Fraternity Of Man whose classic dopers' anthem, 'Don't Bogart That Joint' had graced the soundtrack to the era's most celebrated movie, Easy Rider. Paul's choice of kit was Slingerland — 'noisy, but the best-sounding drums' — and he was soon adding a much-needed edge to his new band. Winter-Hart's early endeavours included a spell with Naked, who later became Reef.

The group underwent the usual metamorphoses — members left, names changed, but Paul was fascinated by what he'd got himself into. He was living in a windowless bedsit in Chiswick and having a miserable time. He shared his accommodation with a group of bus drivers who were doing coke and heroin, one of whom told Paul so convincingly that he'd never make a living from music that he took the test to be a bus driver, only to fail it.

Happily, his new band mates gave him reason for hope. He was suspicious of Alonza because he was too handsome and he smoked Marlboro cigarettes, but the Objects could play and they had good songs. The band served a hard apprenticeship playing all the usual holes in West London and chopped and changed its way through a dozen names from the Lovely Lads to the New Originals. It was to be their singer Saul Dismont — Crispian's handsome cousin — who finally put the group on to the road of enlightenment.

It was he who turned their minds on to the quasi-spiritual direction, they'd always secretly hankered after — it was Dismont who told them about the magical letter 'K', a symbol that was common to more contemporary knights such as Kennedy. Finally they settled on the Kays — a fitting monicker for a posse of wannabe knights. After all hadn't Sir Kay been one of the inner circle of the Grail-seekers and Arthur's talkative brother?

However, Crispian had hit rut city and decided to go to India. It was 1993. He'd become increasingly fascinated with the East through his conversations with erstwhile band mate Marcus Maclaine, a Hare Krishna follower and boyfriend of mum Hayley.

Goa, the much-favoured haunt of the jet-set rave culture, wasn't part of the itinerary — like the other members of the Kays — this scene was total anathema to him. 'I was dragged along to a rave once and I swear I thought it was like people dancing into the mouth of death,' observed the singer.

First stop was Delhi, where he got a job in a temple, exchanging general work for

food and a place to sleep. The pilgrimage then continued down to Orissa and up to Calcutta, meeting holy men and receiving spiritual insights.

It was there that Crispian first got the vision to fuse ethnic Indian music with conventional rock sounds. On his travels he also heard the heady chanting in the ancient tongue of Sanskrit – known as 'the language of the gods' – and decided to incorporate that into the songs he was writing.

He returned with a purpose. Setting up a loose commune with Paul and Alonza firstly in Swiss Cottage, later in Cricklewood and finally in Highgate, the trip began to come together. Already on the scene was the band's 'madness guru', Don Pecker, an ex-jailbird and taxi-driver who looked and acted like Fagin to Crispian's Artful Dodger, hence the nickname of 'Dodge'! Mills had met Pecker in a Krishna Temple.

Pecker had all the right credentials. In the 1960s he'd been close with the god-like genius singer Scott Walker, who had been a major influence on everyone from Julian Cope to Jarvis Cocker. This colourful ex-paratrooper was a big influence on the band and his larger-than-life exploits made a big impression on Crispian.

Pecker had been banged up in Wormwood Scrubs for GBH – and, while doing his porridge, he'd discovered that he was a descendant of the knights of the Holy Grail! It was a significant omen.

Another visitor to their commune was the mysterious Mathura whom Crispian had known since Hampton days – according to Mills, Mathura had been variously a 'Far Eastern informer', a monk and a 'revolutionary conspirator'. Mathura helped Crispian study the teachings of the ancient holy Indian mystic whose name was Chaitanya.

With all these heavy influences in their minds, they packed into Pecker's sleek green Mercedes and headed off on some adventures that led to them playing at the 1993 Glastonbury Festival. The Mercedes had apparently been given to Pecker by an Indian man, who informed him that his guru had said that Pecker was going to save the world and, incredibly, to hand the car over to him! In addition the Indian gave him £13 pounds a week to maintain the machine – in Kula Shaker's world of coincidence and numerology the number was to become super-significant, appearing everywhere.

The car's previous owner had apparently been decapitated in a nasty incident at the Knobs & Knockers hostelry in the Finchley Road and somehow the car had been reported stolen. So there were Mills and Pecker trucking down the road under the influence of some extremely potent acid when the Somerset highway patrol pulled them over. Pecker's gift of the gab persuaded the policemen that he and Crispian weren't the crooks

they were looking for and that anyway, they couldn't be arrested because they were protected by the magic powers of the number 13. The pair were eventually released at exactly 13.13. Crispian sought out the rest of the band and they played an hour or so of 'distorted acid rock' in the Hare Krishna tent at Worthy Farm, including an early version of 'Govinda', which would become Kula Shaker's fourth single.

The Kays began to build up a sizeable following in West London but the music wasn't happening and it was time to ring some changes. Singer Saul Dismont was ushered out. A Lenny Kravitz-type figure whom their then manager saw as the band's focal point, Saul had a major drawback – he'd only play gigs in central London. When they played elsewhere, Crispian would sing – he

had a good voice – and soon enough Alonza suggested that Mills should front the band full-time, an opportunity he seized with alacrity. Once Saul had departed to run the Blow Up club, the manager lost interest too and did a bunk, but it was around this time that the final piece in the jigsaw fell into place.

Enter keyboard player Jay Darlington, a Taurean born on 3 May 1969. With Jay's arrival almost pre-empting Saul's ejection, the music changed substantially from the 'dodgy funk stuff' they'd been playing. The Kays had been nominally part of the West London Mod scene. Since the late 70s when bands like the Jam and Merton Parkas had recharged the batteries of this youth subcult, which enjoyed its heyday in the early 60s, there has always been a Mod movement. Mods like sharp clothes and the Kays were no exception – indeed Crispian suffers from damaged tendons in his feet from being a fashion slave to Cuban-heeled boots! And if you study the current image of Kula Shaker, you'll see that the band eschew the florid kaftans, flares and other regalia usually associated with the late 60s – aside from the token love beads – for smart suits, striped shirts and drainpipe pants.

Darlington came from a very Mod background and fitted in immediately with the band's spiritual image. His mother was a psychic, and Jay claimed he grew up in a heavily haunted house in Battersea! Like Crispian he loved the

Kinks whom he discovered as a youngster when he came across a box of old singles from the 60s in the family attic. Interestingly, one of the Kinks' most loved songs, 'See My Friend' was written in 1965 after leader Ray Davies had heard Indian fishermen singing while working on fixing their nets. The shape of Kula things to come!

Jay subsequently played in various combos in Kent in between spells as a milkman. Kent has always been a Mod stronghold – back in the early 80s there was one band in particular from that culture who looked set to hit the big time, the Prisoners.

Jay was a big fan, especially of their organist, who went on to success as the leader of the eponymous James Taylor Quartet. He was also very comfortable with the 60s tag. Jay played in a variety of bands including the Sheds, who later metamorphosed into the great garage beatsters the Mystreated, and with his trusty Vox Continental (with the black and white keys reversed) gigged with London-based Mod/psyche aggregation Tilt-A-Whirl and even had a brief spell with retro popsters, the Aardvarks. The connection didn't end there – Jay still shares a place with Aardvark Jason, whose girlfriend also has the job of designing Kula Shaker's snappy duds.

Jay arrived in the Kays camp with a thatched bowl haircut and Crispian's first impression of the keyboard maestro was a strange one. Amusingly, Crispian thought that Jay was wearing a German tank helmet when he first saw him. So intrigued was the would-be singer that he went to investigate, only to discover it was really Jay's hair.

Later Jay remembered the days of the bowl haircuts, something that both he and Crispian shared long before they met, contrary to all 1980s fashions. Surprisingly the organist didn't join the rest of the bunch in the commune and, equally surprising, the others tolerated his day job as a graphic designer in a publishing company, which he hung on to until two months after Kula Shaker had signed to Sony!

The Kays soldiered on 'playing crappy pub gigs' while at home they took on a stiff diet of Indian classical music – the sound they were seeking began to take shape. They even landed a support spot for BBM, the 'supergroup' featuring Jack Bruce, Ginger Baker and Gary Moore.

In 1994 the Kays hooked up with Gut Records. Although as an indie label Gut Records couldn't pour large sums of money into the band, label boss Guy Holmes foresaw that Crispian was going to be a huge star and encouraged the group to make better demos and do as much live work as possible. The group went into the studio under the guiding hand of Giles Martin, son of the more famous producer and Beatles' right-hand man, Sir George.

According to Paul, the recordings were straight pop, less garagey and less Indian, though Guy Holmes maintains that the music they were playing back then didn't change too much afterwards. Unfortunately Gut Records fell out with their then manager, who was eager to get on with releasing records – not part of Holmes' immediate plan.

The Kays subsequently left the company but, three years on, Holmes harbours no bad feelings other than he wishes his company could have retained the group.

However it was a huge disappointment for the band, whose morale ebbed to an all-time low. Towards the end of 1994 they played at the Leisure Lounge in London. Crispian remembers, 'The support act was some guy who hung irons and swords from his dick. He played real loud techno while his naked girlfriend smoked crack on stage. We finally went on at about four in the morning to this half-empty room of people coming down from smack. We've got these Indian backing tracks, singing about the sunrise, and there's this bunch of naked guys in the audience shouting, "When are you going to start buggering each other?" That was a low point . . .'

The spring of 1995 was a grim time. The band had just broken from Gut Records, and felt they'd been badly treated. In their shared house, tension was rising; there was a hatch from the kitchen into the living room and on one occasion Crispian threw everything he could find through the hatch at Paul. During this period things were so bad that on New Year's Eve after busking in Soho, Alonza, Paul and Pecker set off on a tour of Southern Europe in Crispian's little camper van – taking a couple of electric guitars and Pignose amps together with Paul's snare, little tom and cymbal, they headed for North Africa for some fun. 'We only got as far as Malaga', Paul recalled, 'we played outside this sombre Catholic shrine doing "Spirit In The Sky" and we didn't get a penny that day, the pilgrims didn't get the irony of it.'

Back in London help from a higher plane was called for. At the end of 1993, Mathura had visited the band's Swiss Cottage pad with an American friend, an original follower of Krishna and someone who'd lived with John Lennon. His name was Kula Sekhara, and he regaled the band with exciting tales deep into the night. He explained how the the original Kula Sekhara was a ninth-century mystic and emperor, and the band, feeling that they needed a bit of regal patronage, took his name in the hope that he would look after them.

The new name fitted the band's continuously improving Indo-rock fusions like a glove, since Kula Shaker were beginning to incorporate Eastern ragas more and more into their heavy retro-rock.

Of course they weren't the first musicians to look eastwards for inspiration – jazz musos like John Coltrane had been doing it in the 50s, but 'raga-rock' had first appeared on record through the hip small US label ESP. In 1964 they recorded a New York band 'Seventh Sons' led by fringe rocker

Buzzy Linhart in a loft in Baltimore and the subsequent improvisational 'Raga' made an indelible mark. But it was the Byrds who started the craze for ragas when Roger McGuinn got out their electric Rickenbacker 12-string guitar and married the droning sound of Indian sitar-maestro Ravi Shankar with the sonic athleticism of John Coltrane's sax improvisations to create 'Eight Miles High', a song with a sound so deliriously weird and different that both 'raga-rock' and 'psychedelic rock' became new genres overnight.

For rock musos it then became open-season – Paul Butterfield's amazing 'East–West' improvs on Elektra Records took it further, while George Harrison spent his remaining years in the Beatles studying Indian mysticism and incorporating both the sitar and Indian ragas into the Fab Four's increasingly complex music. It started with 'Norwegian Wood' and by the time of Sgt Pepper had infiltrated the group's sound as a whole.

Come the Summer of Love in 1967 and every serious rock band had to feature the droning sound of this traditional stringed Indian instrument. Coral even patented an electric version of this usually acoustic instrument in the USA. Groups like the Incredible String Band were particularly adept at absorbing the sitar into their music and one band especially, Traffic, enjoyed big hits like 'Paper Sun' as a result.

As the 60s wore on, musicians became more serious, and key figures started to follow Indian religion – the Fab Four and Donovan went off to meditate and study under the Maharishi, while the Small Faces' Ronnie Lane and the Who's Pete Townshend experienced spiritual epiphanies and ended up as followers of the avatar Meher Baba whose philosophy was crystallized as simply, 'Don't Worry – Be Happy'.

But perhaps Kula Shaker's true antecedents were a British six-piece band who led a deeply spiritual and communal existence in West London's hippy

paradise, Notting Hill Gate. Quintessence attempted to fuse white rock with Indian sounds and religion and their gigs, often free, were righteous uplifting tribal gatherings. Live, the band would improvise, opening with 'Ganga Mai', an invocation of the goddess of water, with their singer Shiva Jones chanting holy mantras, while their lead guitarist Allan Mostert was one of the era's most skillful wah-wah merchants, taking off on wild liberating flights of fancy.

The band recorded five albums, the first three of which for Island Records boasted some of the most elaborate artwork ever used in a rock context and wallowed in all things Indian. Britain in the late 60s seemed to embrace the East harder than most Western countries and even the Radna Krishna Temple enjoyed some Top 50 success with a a brace of 45s on the Beatles' own Apple label. Meanwhile other bands like the Magic Carpet with Clem Alford's electric sitar to the fore also explored the East–West musical interface.

Neither punk nor 80s synth pop could completely kill off the sitar and a whole line of psychedelic bands from the Soft Boys and the Teardrop Explodes to the Rain Parade and Plasticland kept its sound in the public eye. The magnificent Monsoon featuring singer Sheila Chandra brought Indo-pop back in the charts in April 1982 with the fabulous 'Ever So Lonely', a biryani of Eastern pop spices swathed in a mist of sitars and weeping strings, reached Number 12.

More recently the Modfather himself, Paul Weller, took up this stringed instrument for his highly-acclaimed Wild Wood album and for a little known release for record label Virgin France where, billed as Indian Vibes, (alongside Brendan Lynch and Marco Nelson), Weller plucked sitar in time to a jazz favourite, 'Mather'. Kula Shaker don't actually use a sitar in their recordings nor do they sample the sound of one – to create that glistening whiff of the Orient that drifts magically through their music like honeysuckle incense, they

use a simpler version of the instrument called the tampura.

Patronage from the great Indian chieftain seemed to do the trick. Early in 1995, Kula Shaker started to find themselves increasingly in demand and continually out on the road. Firstly they supported old mates Reef and then found themselves on a university tour with Corduroy, a band whose former incarnation, Boys Wonder, Alonza had been a big fan of. The dates with Reef however weren't always easy, as the Reef fans, who were mostly surfers, didn't even know who Kula Shaker were. In-between hauls up and down the motorways, the quartet continued to demo their songs and trawl the record labels for that elusive deal, though their main aim was to win people over with their gigs. Whatever the plan, that longed-for break was just around the corner . . .

A new Svengali figure now entered the Kula Shaker story in the shape of Kevin Nixon – and he'd already managed to interest RCA in funding yet more demos, while interest from other major companies was mounting. The band entered the music industry's 1995 In The City competition funded by north-western brewery Boddingtons, which aims to discover the best unsigned act of the year.

Fifty-seven hopefuls applied and in September 1995 Kula Shaker found themselves up in Manchester playing the finals before a panel of judges that included ex-Wah! frontman Pete Wylie, New Order's Peter Hook and Lightning Seed Ian Broudie. In the event, Kula Shaker tied as joint-third winners with Placebo and Performance for a £3000 prize donated by the Manchester Airport Authority.

One of the onlookers that fateful night was Dave Massey of Hit & Run

Music Publishing, who would subsequently sign the quartet. He had already heard a demo tape of six songs and had fallen in love with 'Under the Hammer' after hearing only 30 seconds of it.

This was the first opportunity he had had to see them live. On a wet Manchester night, only about 100 people had turned out to see them, but afterwards there was a queue for them. Everybody from Hit & Run loved them. The owner of Hit & Run later likened the experience to seeing the Rolling Stones at the Station Hotel in the 60s.

The group did subsequently sign their songs to Hit & Run, at what was picked as an auspicious time – 4.58 pm on 13 November 1995.

Someone else who was mad for them was Columbia A&R man Ronnie Gurr. Gurr had heard reports of live magic and when Kevin Nixon played him the tape done for RCA, he was hot to trot. He was set to sign them but first he had to see them live. Gurr was also present on that fateful Manchester night

and was duly impressed, as he told *Music Week*: 'They can write pop songs, they have substance and they have an experimental edge – a few eastern influences, dance sounds, 60s influences, even Manchester baggy sounds.'

After trouncing the opposition at 'In The City' Kula Shaker were in an enviable position and were swiftly courted by other major labels, but Gurr and Columbia (and parent company Sony) won through, setting up a deal in only 12 working days, though apparently the band was more swayed by Columbia's dedication to making them a success than by a huge financial advance. Nixon also favoured the fact that Columbia didn't have anything like Kula Shaker, which meant that the band would have their own space. Columbia wanted to push Kula Shaker by concentrating on building a fan-base before crossing them over into the commercial mainstream, and envisaged that their alternative sales force would play a significant part in breaking the band. However, for a band that prided itself on

into the deep

retaining its artistic freedom to act and play as it saw fit, surely signing to a Japanese-owned mega-corporation was the kiss of death? After all Oasis had done pretty well by sticking with an indie label. But Kula Shaker took the view that the vehicle for the modern-day minstrel is the multinational record company, which can spread a message across the world like no one else. Plus the band was convinced ultimately by the number of Sony's address – a significant Number 10 in Great Marlborough Street. Sony wanted to tie the band up to a heavyweight eight-album deal, but the band felt eight was a bit over the top, though they were pleased with the support that Sony was giving them.

Kula Shaker, true to form, chose the date and time of their inking of the Sony contract very carefully. The band later said that they had deliberately signed at an auspicious time when the alignment of the planets was favourable. They then spent hours running around desparately trying to arrange the signing moment for when Jupiter was in conjunction with Mercury. The band, or course, claimed that they weren't in control of the situation, but then neither were Sony . . .

To chill out after signing with 'the Man' and to recharge their karmic batteries for the onslaught of a new era in their fortunes, both Crispian and Alonza sloped off to India in December 1995. Crispian was back there again in February to marry his long-time girlfriend Jo in an ethnic three-hour ceremony. Any bad karma was cast out of the band – souls were purged, heads were cleared. It was the calm before the storm, as 1996 would see Kula's hot brand of joss stick rock go ballistic!

The first stop on the road to find their personal Holy Grail was the release of a debut single on 1 January 1996 – and they weren't going to kow-tow to media conservatism with it either. The sublime 'Tattva' was a blissful taste of the Orient – a Sanskrit mantra aphorism about the relationship between God and the living entity, according to Crispian. The song had had its origins in conversations the blond-haired guitarist had had with two friends. Both had said exactly the same phrase to him in the space of a week. The key words that Crispian was to remember were 'acinta bheda bheda tattva'. The added significance of the conversations were that these friends were on completely different sides of the world, one in America, the other in England. As is Crispian's want, he immediately took this significance to heart.

What immediately set the record apart was that the lyrics were partly sung in Sanskrit – it was a tantra-tastic slice of pungent pop with a Beatles-esque chorus line and dramatic acid rock guitar lines. Sony released 'Tattva' as a CD single and as a limited edition 7-inch single - as it would've been had it come out in the late 60s – backed with the original 'Hollow Man'. Legend had it that only 2000 copies of the 7-inch were pressed.

Though it failed to chart the single created the all-important buzz, and its release won them a couple of top-notch media slots – an appearance on Channel 4's well-regarded White Room TV programme and on Radio One's Mark Radcliffe Show, both hosted by the Mancunian DJ who knows a good psychedelic tune when he hears one! The lads were pretty nervous about their debut Radio One appear-

ance, but they needn't have been – the performances were so blinding that they used some of the stuff to fill out subsequent releases!

It was time to hit the tarmac and Kula played a London gig with the like-minded Mother Earth before landing a nifty support to fellow Columbia recording artists, the Presidents Of The United States Of America. However the label connection was where the similarities ended. The dates went well enough, Kula's retro classicism going down favourably with the headliners' fans. The dates with the Presidents marked the end of their communal living arrangements. Their last abode in North London had turned out better than expected, but as Paul pointed out, three years of living together was enough. Newly-wed Crispian set up home in Bath – 'real Grail country' – and in early spring the singer realized one of his ambitions by visiting another shrine, the German sea port of Hamburg where the Fab Four had once cut their milk teeth.

Columbia's 'alternative sales force' was primed to do the business with Kula's second single, issued on 22 April (the eve of St George's Day). And if their mystic debut waxing had somewhat mystified the media, this new one would surely upset them with its title, 'Grateful When You're Dead', tying Kula's love of the 60s to one of that era's most enduring groups, San Francisco's Grateful Dead, whose mind-zapping jams and easy-going Americana-rock was a dope smoker's nirvana, but the bête noir for any 90s kid brought up on a diet of techno and punk. In fact the song was never intended to be a tribute to the

Californian purveyors of laid-back love'n'peace vibes but a cruel pun that showed that underneath their promotion of all things spiritual lurked a wicked sense of humour.

'Grateful' was a supersonic slice of classic rock borrowing heavily from the Chicago Transit Authority (an American brass-rock ensemble that eventually shortened its name and released dreadful middle of the road hits in the mid-70s). In Kula's hands, the sound was revamped for the new generation, punching in scratchy guitar licks, virile Hammond and even a middle bit that used the melody from the music that heralded the old Pearl & Dean adverts at the cinema in the 60s.

The song itself touched on mortality and reincarnation and the band added a further twist by writing a spacey coda, 'Jerry Was There', that recalled the echoplex delights of another once-loved psychedelic band, Welsh fretboard explorers Man. But was it a bare-faced tribute to the guru of the Gibson guitar, Dead leader Jerry Garcia, who'd

passed on the summer before? Crispian later explained that the band had started playing the track before Garcia died. His Californian cousin is a full-on Deadhead, and like all Deadheads, is a great believer in the Jerry Garcia cult that the legendary man 'knew'. Fans take this so seriously that gets all gets slightly eerie. The song was originally intended to be something of a joke, but when Garcia died the band added 'Jerry Was There' which was about his memorial concert in Golden Gate Park. They knew that the Deadheads would be wandering around getting psychedelic vibes from Garcia's presence. The band claimed they were just tapping into the future, a sort of mystical occurrence drawn from Jerry himself.

Kula Shaker's growing legion of fans could buy the CD which included a radio-edited 'Grateful', the full version of the same track and two other songs. 'Another Life' was also the flip of the limited 7-inch run and found the band in tripping, stoned-out mode with giggling voices and a whiff of tampura before the band broke out into heavy Led Zep riff-city with screaming lead guitar and soaring harmonies. Winter-Hart contributed some tub-thumping as the song faded out.

The bonus cut on the CD was 'Under The Hammer', a song that had been written about their low ebb two years before. Surprisingly, this was a real upper. Again employing a dazzling mixture of bluesy licks and Indian mantras, the tune was strangely reminiscent of American 60s politico legends Steppenwolf, especially Jay's easy-ridin' organ swells, that tipped the cut into an ecstatic orgy of electric music for the mind and body.

'Grateful' had been the song they'd performed on the White Room and though it again failed to chart, it sustained the notion that something was happening – though no-one knew quite yet what it was. Crispian said that they were just as into the other songs on the CD and that 'Grateful' was intended to be something to promote on the tour and that would work well on radio. It was supposed to be a taster, but it took off beyond the band's wildest expectations.

Hot on the heels of its release, the band took their debut bow on MTV. It was an occasion not to be squandered and Kula Shaker, trained by the silver-tongued Don Pecker, used the opportunity to indulge in the first of an on-going series of wind-ups with the media. It was almost surreal – Crispian and Jay were subjected to a barrage of dumb questions from a studio audience before the phone lines opened and enquirers were allowed to fire queries to the coolsome two-some – having qualified by crooning the words to Stevie Wonder's banal hit, 'I Just Called To Say I Love You'.

The pair were asked by one 12-year-old to give advice on getting a band off the ground, and Crispian took the bait. 'The first thing is you go out take a load of psychedelic drugs',

quipped the guitarist, and the studio erupted in the kind of panic normally reserved for the likes of Black Grape on TFI Friday. There's no question that the Kulas advocate the careful use of organic stimulants, though the band are far from united on their stance of euphoriant usage. Paul regards himself as the renegade drinker of the band.

Jay and Crispian meanwhile have both recently allegedly renounced any dependency on the 'green goddess'. However, all do agree on the beneficial effects of a nice cup of tea, the drink first brought back to these shores centuries ago from the Indian colonies. In one interview, when Crispian was asked where the band got its inspiration, he put it down to drinking a lot of tea!

To promote the new single, Kula Shaker toured the clubs of Middle England through May and June 1996 with a vengeance – their star was finally in ascent. While the punters at the Blackwood Miners Institute might now boast over their pint pots, 'we saw 'em first' when the band played at the Tunbridge Wells Forum a month later the media was hot on the trail, even if the vitriol wasn't far behind. A review of this show in Melody Maker remarked that 'grateful when you're in bed' would be more appropriate. Such criticism marked the beginning of a very ambivalent relationship between the band and journalists.

However, all would agree that their showcase gig in London at the 100 Club on Tuesday 21 May was one to remember. It was the one where the hip elite finally sat up and took notice, a night to look back on like when the Sex Pistols erupted there back in 1976 or the Jesus & Mary Chain blew the old Ambulance Hut apart in 1984 or, God forbid, the Pink Floyd's debut at the UFO club in Tottenham Court Road in 1967.

The celebs were out in force, a queue of fans stretching way up Oxford Street and round the block. The 100 Club remains one of London's oldest, friendliest and most intimate of venues – many of rock's old guard have chosen to play low-key gigs there such as the Stones with their now-legendary 1982 shows. Robbie Williams was there, Liam Gallagher allegedly took one look at the line outside and drove home, but even controversial DJ Chris Evans rubbed shoulders with the *hoi polloi*.

Nobody went home disappointed. Kula Shaker shook the foundations, and Jeff Horton, booker at the club, said it was one of the two best gigs down there in 1996 (the other was the Real People from Liverpool). Support band the Daisies warmed up the capacity crowd nicely with their jangling guitar-based power-pop before the headliners tore the place apart. The review in *Sold Out* fanzine reported that Kula Shaker were the most exciting new band around, with their late-60s-style psychedelic rock.

And journalists weren't the only ones frothing at the mouth with superlatives. Chris Evans was straight on the phone to Sony the next morning demanding a tape of tracks so far recorded for their debut album, which he later played and enthralled his early morning audience with.

To fuel the fires of interest, Columbia readied a third single, surprisingly a different version of the first. However, the logic was that the first was a limited-edition 45, just to get the band's name known, and it was now a bit of a collectors' item. 'Tattva' came out on 24 June in a variety of formats including 7-inch single and two different CD versions, and would soon strike gold, hitting the top 4. The timing could not have been better, coinciding with the first blaze of a sweltering English summer.

The clattering tablas — a small Indian hand drum — on it struck the right erotic note. Taking its inspiration from an obscure, 500-year-old Indian maxim, 'the inconceivable simultaneous oneness and difference of reality', proclaimed by an Indian holy man, Chaytanya, it was a glorious, sensuous herald of the sunshine season, floating on a cloud of hallucinatory tampura, erogenous waves of wah-wah guitar and

bathed in Jay's gentle mellotron, which sparkled like a tributary of the Ganges. A perfect backdrop for fun in the sun, it caught the public's imagination.

'Dance In Your Shadow' was an equally elegant ballad, hopelessly Beatles-derived with a melody line very reminiscent of 'Norwegian Wood', but who cared? In the Noel Gallagher era, this was totally acceptable. It was piped softly through the dawn sky with snatches of acoustic guitar, propelled by Jay's dexterous skills on the Hammond. 'Moonshine', meanwhile, was a sturdier beast, a psychedelic pachyderm that had drunk deep at the Harrison waterhole and then prowled through the jungle night with all the purpose of a Hathi on heat.

'Tattva (Lucky 13 Mix)' was deliriously trippy — though maybe not so radio-friendly — with the tabla brought up front to create a swirling raga for the 90s generation, and the whole Kula Shaker Indic trip was reinforced by the sleeve with its postage stamps from the pearl-shaped continent.

But arguably the stand-out cut was a version of Tim Hardin's lament from the late 60s, 'Red Balloon (Vishnu's Eyes)'. The song had been originally recorded for inclusion on a pro-

jected Small Faces tribute LP – Marriott and company had themselves recorded the tune for their last, posthumous album, *The Autumn Stone*. The project had originally been handled by Acid Jazz, who'd just published Paolo Hewitt's Small Faces biography.

Sadly the cut never made the finished tribute waxing, *Long Agos And Worlds Apart*, when it finally came out in September 1996. Released via Nice Records owned by ex-Small Faces drummer Kenney Jones, the song would have fared excellently among tip-of-the-hats from the likes of Ocean Colour Scene, the Buzzcocks, Primal Scream, Paul Weller and Northern Uproar. The Shaker version brought out both the original's folksiness and the passion of the Small Faces reading – Crispian's vocals never sounded so soulful and the band as a whole hunkered down to some heartfelt ensemble playing. Though no reason was officially given for its omission, perhaps the fact that royalties from Long Agos were to benefit multiple sclerosis research and ex-Small Faces bassist Ronnie Lane suffers from the disease meant that a performance of a non-group original had to be vetoed. A pity nonetheless.

The 'Tattva' single was nominated Single Of The Week by a major music weekly, where the reporter gushed wholeheartedly about the roots of the track, likening it to the hedonistic excesses of the late 60s when the common soundtrack was as exotic as the Kula Shaker offering. This era was when the Beatles were focussing on the East; the aggressively sexual Rolling Stones were flirting with the Underworld, a smacked out Jimi Hendrix was hitting new highs and the Doors were explor-

ing a dark narcissism; Kula Shaker established their own rich, dreamy wonderland.

The band was now in demand – there may have been no Glastonbury in 1996 but there was a welter of other outdoor events, most of which Kula Shaker managed to get in on. On 14 July they were up on the boards in Glasgow at T In The Park on the same stage as the Longpigs and Ian McNabb. The NME took the opportunity to round up a bunch of bright young stars appearing there to participate in their Bar Humbug series to debate serious issues of the moment. Who better then than Crispian, the talkative, conspiracy-theorist frontman of Kula Shaker, who cast conversational pearls before swine alongside Dubstar's Sarah Blackwood, Teenage Fanclub's Norman Blake and Crispin Hunt from the Longpigs. Mills was on demon form, observing that Tony Blair was being paid for by America and giving the Masons and the Royal Family a good verbal kicking on the way – concluding with a typical Shaker take on the monarchy, that it is pretty much over unless the monarchy becomes something magical again.

Four days later the Kula camper van was driving through the dust of Shakespeare country to the Phoenix Festival, the annual rock gathering in the Midlands headlined in 1996 by the likes of David Bowie, Neil Young and the re-formed Sex Pistols! The band was in high spirits when they played the opening day, basking in the glow of their Top 5 smash, about which Alonza joked at the Festival that it was 'the guvnor upstairs' who wanted it to be a hit. The band are great believers in fate, and claimed that following little signs like the letter K and

numbers such as 10 and 11, 13 and 33 being good for them was the basis of their success. As well as playing on the Doc Martens stage the lads soaked up the sun and even squeezed in a game of football!

The four riders of the imminent apocalypse headlined their own show at London's Astoria theatre on 2 August, where they blew up a storm of piledriving guitar chords, jazz-tinged bass runs, drumming of an Alpine avalanche intensity and rivers of Hammond organ. The audience lapped it up but the critics were still not convinced by the band's 60s classicism and heart-felt, alternative beliefs.

If the hacks were having trouble, Noel Gallagher wasn't. He invited the band to play at Oasis's Knebworth Park extravaganza on 10 August. Anticipating the great event, Jay said that although Kula Shaker hadn't met them yet Oasis seemed like top lads and they'd love to support them. The guys weren't in the least fazed by having to play to their biggest audience — 125,000 people — thus far. Paul later admitted that he had thrown up from nerves when the band did Hastings Crypt the night before, but from the stage Knebworth had looked like a painting of people rather than a real audience and he hadn't suffered from nerves at all.

Kula Shaker were absolutely delighted to receive the royal invitation from Manchester's answer to Paul McCartney, though Crispian remarked that while Noel Gallagher had been nice about them and was nothing like the image of Oasis, Liam had got a few problems. BBC 2's The O Zone caught up with the band at the Hertfordshire stately home and found that, far from hob-nobbing with all the other stars in an orgy of excess, Alonza and Crispian were quietly searching around — kettle in hand — for some water to brew up in the famed camper van prior to the gig!

As The Fast Show 's Poula Fisch might've said of the weather forecast over southern England for the third weekend of August, it was 'scorchio' when the quartet played a support as part of the Paul Weller fest, V96 in Chelmsford on 18 August. And then it was full steam ahead for the annual Reading bash where they joined Saturday 24th's bill that included Shaun Ryder's Black Grape and space case Julian Cope.

This constant blitz on the public was beginning to pay off — there was a groundswell of interest in the band's forthcoming debut album and to stir things up to a fever pitch on the back of their Reading appearance, Columbia released a new single on 26 August. 'Hey Dude' — a neat pun on the old Beatles song — was the band back in heavier, funkier mode with slashing rhythms, screaming lead guitar lines alternating with slide fills and a dancing back-beat. Crispian's vocals were at their bluesy best while, as ever, Jay's Hammond glued it all together — late 60s British rock meets the Roses. It was an immediate radio favourite and shot up the charts to the Number 2 position, probably helped by a wackily psychedelic promo video that pictured the band driving round London playing on board an open-top double-decker bus!

Like its predecessor, the single came in a variety of formats, though this time, there was no vinyl version. CD 1 also boasted 'Troubled

Mind', a mid-tempo number with pretty acoustic guitars, bolstered by some steaming organ swells and beefy horns behind the chorus and a typically toothsome lead break from Crispian. The disc was completed by two selections from their radio debut on Mark Radcliffe's Show the previous February. If the band was suffering from mild stage fright, they didn't show it – the version of 'Grateful When You're Dead', live in the studio, was raw and unfettered and showed the band's garage roots snarling through.

The version of 'Into The Deep' also featured here was far less polished than the one that would end up on their debut LP – a real hard-headed little mother with Crispian's lead guitar tracing out some pulsating modal arabesques and Paul's drumming driving the tune along at a cracking pace. These performances were certainly the most tribal they'd committed to wax. CD 2 was rounded off with yet another cut from the classic Radcliffe session including some ribald banter between the Mancunian jock and Crispian who had to burst out laughing when Radcliffe suggested that Sham 69 had cut a version of 'Tattva'. The version of their big hit was shorn of its tampura drone but sizzled dreamily, moodily along with some slide playing from Crispian as icily incisive as ever and a fat organ sound.

The rest of this CD was enticingly diverse and imbued the band's oft-criticised one-dimensional retro image with some much-needed depth. 'Drop In The Sea' was enchanting, basically just Crispian and his acoustic, singing a bed-sit ballad that might've fallen straight off the first Leonard Cohen LP. The final track was Crispian reading from The Mahabharata, again from the Radcliffe show with a snatches of 'Tattva' fading in and out of the narrative. As with the previous single, 'Hey Dude' was stylishly packaged with potent images dreamt up by Bayswater graphics company Stylorouge.

Hot on its heels, Kula Shaker were flown over to the States to play some debut live shows. Things didn't quite go off as they should've as Crispian, suffering from the onslaught of travelling and air-conditioning, lost his voice. But in the end the gigs were rocket-fuelled. The band felt they all played well, and found themselves described as 'awesome'. Nevertheless, they were realistic enough to know that just believing they were going to conquer the US meant nothing until they actually did it.

The very idea of the oh-so British Kula Shaker playing in the land of the free and the brave was something to savour, especially with the accent of the band's message so heavily on the spiritual plane – a stark contrast, the Native Americans apart, to that continent's so smotheringly materialistic beliefs. Crispian has expressed the view that while America has shaped the structure of the Western way of making money and its concept of success over the last 50 years, the US position as the leading world power is soon going to be on the wane. He has described it as a civilization based on having as opposed to being, and one that exploits the individual. It will be interesting to see how the Sony-owned band will deal with the American establishment as their fame begins to mushroom.

Thoughts of the US were put to one side when the band flew back to the UK to play the MTV Awards at Alexandra Palace at the beginning of September and simultaneously prepare the way for the imminent release of their debut album. As they prepared to play their 'Tattva' hit at the Awards, Crispian had a special, cryptic message for the MTV audience: 'Dearly beloved, we are gathered here today in the sight of almighty God to kiss the Devil's arse!'

 All through the previous months Kula Shaker had been assembling material for the first album. As they'd sped up and down the highways and byways of Albion, they'd recorded at a number of different studios, fitting sessions in around their busy gig schedule. Some had been produced by Crispian, some under the Shep and Dodge monicker (Bevan and Mills) but it was felt that such an important debut waxing should be produced by the hands of a maestro. Enter John Leckie.

Leckie had become one of the decade's most sought-after producers and had left his mark on albums as revered as *The Bends* by Oxford's Radiohead. Leckie instinctively gets the best out of guitar-orientated bands and will go down in the history books as the man who produced the milestone eponymous debut album by the Stone Roses, and there are many who feel he should have baby-sat the Mancs through their painful *Second Coming*.

Leckie is a veteran with an impressive track record – his first session was as engineer for George Harrison's 'My Sweet Lord' with Phil Spector at the controls – and that was enough of a recommendation in its own right for Crispian and the gang. Leckie subsequently worked with artists as diverse as Pink Floyd and Cast, but another project that must have endeared him to Kula Shaker was his production on the aforementioned Dukes Of Stratosphear.

XTC guitarist Andy Partridge's cod psychedelic wheeze, the Dukes had released two fabbo waxings – 25 O'Clock and Psonic Sunspot – on Virgin in 1985 and 1987 respectively. All the correct period detail was there right down to the mind-blowing sleeve artwork and John Leckie had licked every pastiche from Swinging London Mod rave-ups to San Francisco-style acid rockers into shape. So authentic was the finished product that the LPs curried favour with both original fans of the genre and those who wanted to guffaw down their baggies!

Leckie had heard Kula Shaker's first single, and been impressed. He went to see
them at the Splash Club and the Dublin
Castle and told them he wanted to work
with them, but at the time they had other
plans. Three months later they called him
and said they wanted to start work the
next day.

The timing for the release of the
debut album, K, couldn't have been more
perfect, even on an earthly plane. 1996
was the year that saw no new albums by
Britpop supremos Oasis and Pulp, Blur
had crawled away for a rethink after los-
ing their tag-match with the 'Brothers
Grimm', and even hotly touted young
bucks like Supergrass were going through
the all-pervasive second album syndrome.
Given that Ocean Colour Scene's Mosely
Shoals album in all its 60s retro glory had
been the surprise hit album of the summer, K couldn't fail . . . and it didn't! From
the sleeve there on in, K was a winner –
the magical properties of the eleventh
letter of the alphabet were serving them
well! Vaguely Sgt Pepper-esque, the front

cover was a painting by Dave Gibbons, the chap responsible for some of 2000 AD comic's best graphics. Gibbons, as Peter Blake had done for the Beatles and more recently for Paul Weller by deploying those acts' favourite icons, included a rogues' gallery of individuals whose name began with the letter 'K'.

The god in the centre was Krishna – after his birth this deity was secretly abandoned in some cow-herders' dwellings at Mathura in order to divert the search being made for him by Kamsa, an oppressor who Krishna had been born to destroy and who had been fore-warned of his fate. The goddess next to him in the painting was Radha, and the worship of Krishna virtually included that of Radha, his lover, hence the joint cult of Radha Krishna. The youthful amorous adventures of Krishna with the female cowherders, among whom Radha was one, was a famous feature of The Mahabharata and was viewed as an allegory of the devotees' love for their supreme divine lord.

The flute that Krishna was holding on the cover was significant as it called the young women to come and dance in the moonlight and was said to symbolize the voice of God calling those who hear it away from earthly to the divine pleasures.

Moving round the sleeve clockwise, the watch hanging from the letter 'e' in Shaker was pointing at 10 to 10 – there then followed a parade of the good, bad and the bizarre: actor Danny Kaye; the poet Keats; the late US President John F Kennedy (a pregnant image for conspiracy theorists); a white knight chess piece; actor Ben Kingsley (who immortalized Gandhi); King Kong; and actress Grace Kelly.

kula shaker

Then came Ken Dodd (belatedly getting his call in the credibility stakes with a recent appearance in Ken Branagh's Hamlet); a knight's helmet; keys; Lord Kitchener (an icon of Swinging London in the 60s and one of Sir John Mills's film roles in Young Winston); dancer Gene Kelly in the right-hand bottom corner; African politician Jomo Kenyatta; Karl Marx; Superman's alter ego Clark Kent hovered next to Kitchener's hat; infamous pirate Captain Kidd was under the all-powerful sign of the Number 11; Rudyard Kipling, Victorian writer of Kim and The Jungle Book and popularizer on the Indian subcontinent; former 1960s Soviet President Khruschev; former news-reader Howard Kendall; civil rights leader Martin Luther King; Dave Gibbons's wife; British horror actor Boris Karloff; Kali; actress Katharine Hepburn; Captain Kirk; the Kaiser (another icon of 1960s Carnaby culture); actress Kay Kendall; and finally the all-important kettle to keep the constant supply of tea coming.

The insert was equally lavish with a coloured reversed-negative image of the band, the Kula Shaker logo done in a psychedelic mandala and the lyrics to all the songs. But did the music match up? K started with a statement of intent in 'Hey Dude', a rocking cultural touchstone that told you where they were coming from. The similarly punning 'Knight On The Road' was up next, a blistering hard-rocking tune with some searing heavy-metal guitar riffs and Jay vamping it up on the piano for once. It was hard to believe that

a chap as diminutive as Crispian had such enormous fire-power in those lungs of his.

'Temple Of Everlasting Light' took proceedings into the mystic Indic realms, lighter with tabla, acoustic guitar and soaring harmonies, all darting fire-flies and moonlight — a celestial moment of peace after all the scrunching hard rock. It lead seamlessly into 'Govinda', the song's appearance heralded by screaming peacocks (India's national bird), then came heavenly backing vocals from Gauri and languorous tablas. The band still managed to pack some powerful rock punches with a particularly brutal wah-wah solo from Crispian. 'Smart Dogs' took the temperature back up — a full-on magic carpet ride in the vein of Steppenwolf, though the chorus line melody owed more to the Monkees style of harmonizing. 'Smart Dogs' also cropped up on the Vox Class Of 96 CD given away with the magazine and also featured the likes of bands like Suede, Dodgy and Ash.

'Magic Theatre' was a departure — a gentle, almost melodramatic piece whose melody was more East European than Eastern with subtle electric guitar, Jay's classical piano figures and a faint cymbal wash around the edges. 'Into The Deep' which had already been aired on the 'Hey Dude' single was next — close to the sound Californian psychers the Rain Parade were experimenting with back in 1983, but then that's not surprising given both bands love of ragas and Beatles vocal harmonies! Crispian's

guitar solo was a blinder — assured and dizzingly modal.

'Sleeping Jiva' was the nearest the group got to an all-out authentic Ravi Shankar sound. Wajahat Kahn played the sarod, a North Indian instrument that sounds like a cross between a slide guitar and a sitar, with four main strings tuned like a violin, four drone strings and 13 sympathetic strings.

An ethereal instrumental piece, 'Sleeping Jiva' heralded the arrival of two of the album's best-known songs, the summer hit 'Tattva' and the complete 'Grateful When You're Dead/Jerry was There'. '303' was an ode to the A-road pilgrims to the annual Glastonbury Festival know so well, with Crispian in self-effacing, send-up mode, 'And I love my hash, yeah got my stash, Think I'll grow myself a big ol' hairy moustache'! The number rolled along on some funky Hendrix-style wah-wah licks -- Crispian even harmon-ising with his guitar at one point — and Waddington's smoking Hammond fills.

For 'Start All Over', the band put on their Rubber Soul hat to cut a cute pop song with an irresistible hook and Crispian once again showcasing his leather-coated larynx. That was a moment of frivolity to be enjoyed before K played out on the portentous 'Hollow Man Parts 1 & 2'. The first section was a stately instrumental with Darlington's textured use of different keyboards redolent of Traffic or Procol Harum at their best, while

Mills's guitar was positively restrained after his orgasmic outbursts on '303'. 'Part 2' featured acoustic guitar and its words about the search for spiritual fulfilment were arguably the most personal and serious Mills had yet committed to record – indeed after the highs of songs like 'Tattva' and 'Grateful', 'Hollow Man' finished the album on a down-beat, reflective note, which may have been the point, given Crispian's avowed intent of stirring up people's awareness and consciousness.

The melancholic note struck by 'Hollow Man' did nothing to lessen the appeal of K and it was destined to become a mega-seller, rocketing to the top of the UK album charts. The public went out in droves to secure its success, yet the critics weren't convinced and K received a baptism of fire from the music press, who

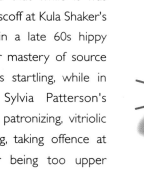 

damned the LP with faint praise.

In the Observer, Neil Spencer said that while it was hard not to scoff at Kula Shaker's absorption in a late 60s hippy heaven their mastery of source material was startling, while in the NME Sylvia Patterson's review was patronizing, vitriolic and grudging, taking offence at Kula Shaker being too upper middle-class before even getting to the music.

The class back-stabbing was something not even Crispian was prepared for. He had never thought of himself of any class, he said – if you were from a thespy home you weren't really in a class because people come to that from all sorts of backgrounds.

However, even NME had to conclude that the middle class boys had triumphed, giving K a stonking 9 out of 10. Ironically Savage Pencil's witty pen-sketch of Kula Shaker that accompanied this review caught the mood far better! However, it was Andy Gill in the Independent who hit the nail on the head. Reviewing both K and the Boo Radley's C'mon Kids, he wasn't convinced by either band's reliance on the past, though he had to concede that Kula Shaker would be internationally massive. It was in his other review

of the page, that of the Pere Ubu box-set Datapanik In The Year Zero, that he saw the flaw in K, saying that the Datapanik actually contained some of the most harrowing music ever made, and that Kula Shaker could learn a lot from these five CDs.

There was the rub — on the down side K was just simply too polished, too safe and unlike the experimental Ubu left nothing to chance and lacked the tribal heart-beat that had informed the best work of the Woodstock generation. The production, too, was John Leckie at his Radiohead sheen worst rather than Stone Roses garagey best — that looser, more primal sound that made 'What The World Is Waiting For' so damn magical and human was this rawer, rougher technique that should have been applied to parts of K.

No matter, Kula Shaker were now public property — 'Tattva' was even heard playing on the radio in Alma and Gail's caff in Coronation Street.

Banners were to be unfurled, the armour for a road campaign to be polished and prepared. After playing the opening night of the Top Of The Pops weekend at Wembley with bands like Ocean Colour Scene, an autumn British tour was just the tonic to maintain K' s pole position in the national chart. Not even a derogatory article in Time Out entitled 'Dad Rock', a survey of the current Brit guitar band wave that likened the 90s to the 60s turned on its head, could stop the momentum. It was a full-house, 13-date haul

culminating in a London gig at the Kilburn National on Wednesday 9 October, though according to some like the NME, it wasn't quite living up to the expectations excited by Crispian's bleatings in the media.

Undeterred by continuing press resistance, the band undertook its first proper tour on the Continent to tell our European cousins that like back home, it was time to get their houses in order. As Hamburg, Berlin and a dozen other cities fell to their celestial charms and raga rock, Crispian was in an uncompromising mood about the critical backlash. 'We didn't think we'd get any support in the beginning because we're so in contrast to everything else around us. But we thought we'd just be ourselves and be laughed at. And we were. It's not about trying to be weird or wacky or sensational, it's about trying to communicate positive magic, hope, idealism, mystery which life is full of. I'm not into singing about the basic, boring side of life. I'm into a bit of mystery'.

The mid-90s ideologies of the E-generation still had a lot of catching up to do with Kula Shaker's 21st-Century visions, but Crispian was unmoved, saying that soon people would realize that the band had been right all along. It was time to take the message back to the smug hinterlands of middle-America – but prior to touching down on American soil, the band recorded a special appearance on the 50th edition of Later With Jools Holland where they rubbed shoulders with Orbital, Blue Nile and two of rock's elder statesmen, Jackson Browne and Joe Cocker.

The occasion was a special thrill for Paul Winter-Hart, who got to meet veteran sticksman Jim Keltner behind the traps for the Sheffield vocalist. A mutual bond of respect quickly formed between the two men, and Keltner wanted Paul to play in his son's band!

By the date of its transmission Kula Shaker were already locked into a 12-date tour of North America, playing in clubs to audiences of anywhere between 500 and 1,200 people each night. US radio had been hugely supportive of the 'Tattva' single and the record was conspicuous in both Billboard's modern rock tracks chart and in Gavin's alternative listings.

The West Coast dates included a gig at the legendary Whisky-A-Go-Go club in West Hollywood where in the 60s such legends as Love and the Doors had first taken off. Sadly the ghost of Jim Morrison was nowhere to be found when the quartet rocked its tiny stage, and Paul described it as a shit-hole. Even a wander down San Francisco's Haight Street, once linked with all those powerful peace'n'love 60s vibes, failed to impress them.

If Jerry was there, he was keeping schtum. However, a rendezvous at the local Live 105 radio station where Alonza and Crispian performed a live acoustic version of 'Govinda' was more enervating and the gig at Slim's on 11th Street was a stormer, despite Jay's organ threatening to give up the ghost during the soundcheck. The 750-fan-packed club celebrated their arrival in the Golden Gate city with a party-like reception, cheering when the band dutifully trotted out its hit singles and most of the album. A week off allowed the band to enter the studio for the first time since finishing K and the sessions in LA overseen by Stephen Harris, who'd engineered some of the tracks on the LP like 'Temple Of Everlasting Light', were regarded by the band as some of the best yet.

From the West Coast it was a plane ride across the Pacific to make their debut in the Land of the Rising Sun. K had been released there in slightly different format with a bonus track. 'Ragey One' was a spacey gem, lit by a rainbow of Crispian's best echoplexed guitar – it was a perfect altar on which the Kula Shaker pilgrims could rest their weary heads, to be bathed in the healing waters of Jay's mesmerizing keyboards and Mills's hallucinatory lead lines. One of their finest, it was a shame it hadn't been included on the UK release.

'Ragey One' was also lined up to appear on the soundtrack to The Saint starring Val Kilmer, and the band also had two tracks, as yet unidentified, scheduled for another film, Nightwatch. The album had already racked up a healthy 150,000 sales by the time the group walked out on to the stage of the Imperial Hall in Osaka on Friday 29 November. Japan fell easily under the band's spell and further dates at the Club Quatro in Nagoya and the Liquid Room in Tokyo were a resounding success. Japanese fans could also rejoice in a special CD version of the 'Grateful When You're Dead' single that brought together some of the sundry tracks that had lurked on the mind-boggling array of varying UK single releases, and was beautifully packaged in the same artwork that had graced the by-then exceedingly rare first single, 'Tattva'.

Back home things had been far from quiet – a fourth single, 'Govinda', from the album had been released right on the numerically correct cue of 11/11/96. As ever, it was available in a variety of formats including a limited edition 7-inch vinyl edition which, due to technical problems, had to play at 33 rpm. All sleeves featured the magnified face of a wrist-watch, crackling with white energy, the hands pointing to 10 to 10 and the date dial set to the number 13!

Above: The Prodigy

CD 1 featured the John Leckie-produced version of 'Govinda', a live version of 'Hey Dude' culled from the Astoria show and a crazy snip of madness lifted from Collins and Maconie's Hit Parade radio show, where Alonza – rather badly, it had to be said – answered questions on the national dish of Wales, the leek. CD 2 featured 'Govinda, Hari and St George' and two further mixes of the song done by the Monkey Mafia – aka Heavenly Records maverick trip-hop DJ John Carter, who'd scored with singles like 'The Dollar' and 'Work Mi Body'.

The Monkey Mafia had come into existence in June 1995 when Carter was enjoying a conversation with Barry from Deja Vu on the concept of 'moon monkeys'. The two mixes here were allegedly taken away from the Mafia before they could turn them into a big beautiful mash up, but the possibilities of Kula Shaker's mantric muse making the cross-over into the clubs was awesomely apparent.

However, the cut that grabbed the headlines was 'Gokula', which had been originally intended for K. The tune was based on a guitar riff on 'Ski-ing', a cut on George Harrison's 1968 Apple masterpiece, Wonderwall. With the Beatles' publishing company Northern Songs maintaining a blanket ban on the usage of the Fab Four's music, both collectively and solo, for anything but cover versions, it looked like the recording would have to remain in the can. Undeterred, Crispian then contacted Harrison through a personal letter which also conveyed Mills's deep-seated Indian beliefs. The Deep One relented, thus creating a little bit of Beatles history, it being the first time a Beatle's song had officially been used in this way. And the cut was a cracker, showcasing once again what an assured and exciting axe-maestro the young Capricorn was – playing with all the fire of a Clapton in his Cream heyday.

Predictably, the 'Govinda' single – sung wholly in Sanskrit – scorched the UK Top 10, reaching Number 7. It was aided and abetted by the band's most accomplished promo video to date. Directed by M. Geoghegan, with its powerful Indian images including the young Krishna playing his flute, it showed the band performing on a lake, consumed by fire and then purified by the rain.

When the band returned to British soil in early December, they could barely stop to draw breath. They'd never forged the bonds of friendship that seemingly held many of the Britpop bands together. Bands like Gene had publicly ridiculed their 'retro' sound. Their values hardly coincided with those held by Kula Shaker, but a note of accord had been struck between Crispian and Cast singer, John Power. Indeed, the band's last hit single, 'Flying' used a psychedelic promo video with a miniature UFO, a definite Kula influence!

Kula Shaker saw 1996 out in a blur of activity – admirer Chris Evans invited them back on his TFI Friday show on the 13th December where they performed '303', while a few days before they'd been given two half-hour slots on MTV in the form of a rockumentary 'The Essential Kula Shaker'. Here, amidst video clips, the lads talked about their origins, their religious beliefs and plans for the future, and 'Live'N'Loud', a live performance that saw them run through a batch of what had by now become big favourites. Jay and Crispian were even espied doing a late-night link for Channel 4 TV.

As Christmas approached, Crispian, Jay and Alonza embarked on what was now becoming a traditional seasonal pastime – a return to their spiritual roots in India to get their karmas in working shape for what promised an even busier new year. The debut album had turned up amongst the year's best in many

journalists' Top 20s, but it was John Leckie who copped the first proper award, as best producer for K at the annual Q magazine awards ceremony. The trophy was presented by ex-Take That singer Mark Owen, himself hoping to be on the receiving end of the Leckie Midas touch in 1996.

Although there was no new record to promote, Kula Shaker were scheduled to play a nine-date UK tour in January. Before they bundled into the tour bus, Alonza and Crispian had a date to keep with the Melody Maker to review the week's batch of new singles. Predictably the pair found little inspiration in the selection they were given and trashed offerings by everyone from the Boo Radleys to George Michael. Ultimately Crispian plumped for a 7-inch by New Zealand indie thrashers the Flakeheads, 'Anaesthetic's In My Brain'. Alonza, meanwhile, loyally chose the latest from old mates Reef, 'Come Back Brighter'.

However, one of Crispian's comments outraged rival organ Time Out , which already had the knives out for the band. Reviewing KRS-1s 'Word Perfect', the guitarist had bemoaned that he wasn't into that stereotyped 'black bitch thing' and turned off automatically when he heard it. He even said that gangsta rap wasn't really even music but just an attitude ego thing. In the following week's Sleevenotes column, the politically correct Time Out

queried whether racism comes from ignorance or stupidity, or possibly both, before taking Mr Mills to task for his review and accusing him of 'tarring all black rappers with his magical twat brush'.

A couple of days later Crispian found himself at the centre of an even more contentious debate – the media war on pop stars and drugs. Following Liam Gallagher's coke bust on Oxford Street and East 17's Brian Harvey's vilification for his comments on ecstasy, the Evening Standard was gunning for the Kula Shaker singer. Under the headline 'A Load Of Tosh From Mr Posh?' Mills' bloodlines and supposedly silver-spooned background were again under attack, and it was said that he could get away with admitting the use of drugs where Brian Harvey couldn't simply because of his greater sophistication and his ability to make drug use seem acceptable within a culture of eastern mysticism.

Fortunately Crispian could absorb himself into the all-important music-making when the tour kicked off at the Manchester Apollo on the 16th – and by the time the band played at the Doncaster Dome two nights later, the golden-haired one was cheered by a spontaneous outburst of his fans singing 'Happy Birthday' to him.

The two dates at the Brixton Academy on 23rd and 24th January were

eagerly anticipated. The Friday show revealed most of Kula Shaker's strengths and one or two flaws. As the white drapes fell back to expose an elaborate stage set, the band filed on at 9.30pm exactly and drove straight into a daring rendition of 'Baby You're A Rich Man' – one of the Fab Four's more Eastern outings – with a superb slide show bouncing potent images behind of them of Lord Kitchener, Krishna and Radha.

It was then time for some tunes from the hit album and after 'Knight On The Road', '303' was the first indication that the band could turn on the heat. A portrait of St George Harrison heralded the next number – an ear-burning 'Gokula' with the sparrow-like Crispian leaping upon the drum podium. 'Grateful When You're Dead/Jerry Was There' showed that as a live number, it left the studio version still-born, with Mills' savage solos invoking the ghost of St Garcia, an image of whom pulsated on the backcloth. It surely won't be long before Mills is talked of in the same hushed tones of reverence as other latterday axe heroes such as John Squire or Blur's Graham Coxon.

A huge psychedelic crescendo ushered in a couple of songs newish to UK audiences, the heavenly 'Ragey One' and the as-yet-unreleased 'For This Love'. The promised acoustic set failed to materialize, the whole band falling in behind Mills for the ballad, 'Drop In The Sea'. 'Tattva' was less Indian than expected,

slower yet more mesmeric than on the hit single — and heavier, with Bevan pulling off some staggering nimble jazz runs on his bass.

'Smart Dogs' and 'Dance In Your Shadow' followed, to be topped by the Number 2 hit 'Hey Dude'. The 13-song set finished with arguably the evening's finest moment, Crispian cryptically announcing 'this might be the new single' as the band launched itself hot-bloodedly into the old Joe South song 'Hush', which had been a minor hit for the pre-In Rock Deep Purple. Obviously a doff-of-the-cap to Mills's old mentor Ritchie Blackmore, the song was tailor-made for Kula Shaker — the 'oh suits you sir' surging Hammond attack, the savage wah-wah guitar and the catchy 'nah nananah' chorus will undoubtedly launch it straight to the top of the charts if plans to release a live version materialize.

The audience — while far from rabid — lured the band back from a

three-pronged encore of 'Hollow Man', 'Into The Deep' and finally 'Govinda', with Mills slipping in snatches of Cream's 'I Feel Free'! And then they were gone. Musically it had been as tight as anything this scribe had seen but Crispian's words came back to haunt me. He said that while its great to be Number 1 and everyone feels like they've achieved something, Peter Andre was the man at the top of the charts. He went on to say that being Number 1 doesn't mean anything unless the music has been used to inspire people in a positive way. That's what Kula Shaker is all about, not just about wanting to be Number 1.

At the end of the Brixton Academy show, there wasn't the euphoria in the air of a classic show. It was just as Johnny Cigarettes had moaned after the Kilburn gig last October — the band had failed to engage. It was one thing for Kula Shaker to assume the spiritual mantle of late-1960s rock and another if they cannot deliver the same kind of tribal communication which bands like the

Who and the Experience could conjure
up almost every night. That joyous
moment when audience and band
become one – forget the ego bullshit and
let the spirit flow.
The year of 1997 will undoubtedly see
Kula Shaker reach bigger heights yet –
they're already nominated for a Brit Award
for Best Album. And they've at least a year
before the armageddon that Crispian so
sincerely predicts – it'll be June '98 when
it all starts going off in Pakistan, China and
India. The band return to the States in
February and April and are scheduled to
play the closing day of the Glastonbury
Festival on 28 June – it should be a tran-
scendental occasion so long as the band
do more than just astrally project themselves! If, as Crispian believes, Britain 'is a
mystical island which has got sleeping energy specifically designed in saving the world
in its darkest hour', then rest assured Kula
Shaker will take rock'n'roll gloriously into
the 21st Century when they play that
promised gig at the foot of the Great
Pyramid on 31 December 1999!

SINGLES:
Tattva/Hollow Man
CD Single KULA CD1 Columbia
7" Single KULA 71 Columbia
Released 1/1/96

Grateful When You're Dead
CD Single KULACD2 Columbia (Grateful When You're Dead (Edit)/
Grateful When You're Dead-Jerry Was There/
Another Life/Under The Hammer
7" Single KULA 72 Columbia (Grateful When You're Dead-Jerry Was There/Another Life)
MC Single KULAMCD2 Columbia
Released 22/4/96

Tattva
CD Single KULACD3 Columbia (Tattva/Dance In Your
Shadow/Moonshine/Tattva (Lucky 13 Mix)
CD Single KULACD3K Columbia (Tattva On St George's Day/Dance In
Your Shadow/ Red Balloon (Vishnu's Eyes)
7" Single KULA 73 Columbia (Tattva/Tattva On St George's Day/
Dance In Your Shadow)
Released 24/6/96

Hey Dude
CD Single KULACD 4 Columbia (Hey Dude/Troubled Mind/Grateful
When You're Dead/Into The Deep)
CD Single KULACD4K Columbia (Hey Dude/Tattva/Drop In The Sea/
Crispian reading From The Mahabharata
MC Single KULAMCD4 Columbia
Released 26/8/96

Govinda
CD Single KULACD5 Columbia (Govinda(Radio Mix)/Gokula/Hey Dude Live At The Astoria/The Leek)
CD Single KULACD5K Columbia (Govinda, Hari and St George/Gokula/
Govinda (Monkey Mafia Pigsy's Vision)/
Govinda (Monkey Mafia Ten To Ten)
7" Single KULA 75 Govinda (Radio Mix)/Gokula/ Temple Of Everlasting Light
MC Single KULAMC5 Govinda (Radio Mix)/Gokula
Released 11/11/96

ALBUM:
K
CD Album SHAKER1CD Columbia
CD Album (digi-pack) SHAKER1CDK Columbia
12" Album SHAKER1LP Columbia
MC Album SHAKER1MC Columbia
Released 16/9/96

Picture credits
RETNA:
Aki 8, Tim Auger 17, 24, 46, 56-57, 59, Steve Double 26, 75,
King Collection 19, Martyn Goodacre 44, 45, 51, 52, 60, Phil Loftus 10, Photofest 19, Joe Ramsey 41, RIP 69, Niels Van Iperen 11
ALL ACTION:
ve Hogan 34, Suzan Moore 21, 40, 42, 62, 66, 69, 76, 77, Ellis O'Brien 20, 22, 23, 29, 43, 63, 64, 65, 68, 72 Doug Peters 6, 7, 24, 32, 33, 35, 39, 58,
Justin Thomas 9, 18, 24, 30, 31, Lili Wilde 71
REDFERNS:
Mick Hutson 16, Simon Ritter 36, 37, 54, 55
LONDON FEATURES INTERNATIONAL LTD:
27, 34
BIG PICTURES:
Darryn Lyons 8

discography

The publisher would like to thank the following publications for their kind permission to use quotes in this book.
Guitar Magazine 16 • Melody Maker 45, 72 • Music Week 37 • Observer 25 • Q 12, 16 • Time Out 73